Life After a Painful Divorce

L.A.P.D.

LIFE *after* A PAINFUL DIVORCE

by

J.K. SANDERS

. . . .

Library of Congress Control Number: 2009907954
ISBN-10 0983637318
ISBN-13 9780983637318

Book cover, layout and design by Tamara R. Allen
Kreativ Intervention
tallen@kreativintervention.com
www.kreativintervention.com

. . . .

DEDICATION

This book is dedicated to anyone who has survived a
divorce, knows a survivor of divorce or wants
to divorceproof their marriage.

. . . .

. . . .

ACKNOWLEDGEMENTS

To those who influenced me the most,
I offer sincere gratitude:

Bishop Fred and Esther Sanders - my loving parents.
You taught me commitment and persistence.
The words you spoke and continue to speak in my spirit
remind me that this is just the beginning.

My wonderful sons - Jonathan and Joshua.
You bring me joy. The world awaits you, soldiers.

. . . .

. . . .

INTRODUCTION

Current statistics indicate that 40 to 60 percent of all marriages will end in divorce. Whether you disagree or choose to accept this statement, the fact remains: divorce is destroying families worldwide.

This book is MY personal story. After celebrating 13 years of marriage and being blessed with two sons, divorce became my reality. If you are divorced or perhaps going through a divorce, your circumstances may be similar or completely different than mine. Your situation can turn out better or worse than mine. All divorces are different; some are as simple as signing a few papers while others may make you feel like hiring a hit man to take out your soon-to-be-ex-spouse!

My divorce initially left me quite depressed, and to be honest, mad with the whole world over what happened to me. I fought through tears, mood swings, loss of appetite and public embarrassment. I also discovered who my true friends are.

I know many other couples − in and out of the church − who have also experienced divorce. I have seen some people progress after divorce, and others digress by turning to alcohol, drugs, sex and other addictions. Some people chose to give up on love all together or opt for an alternative lifestyle. Some of my divorced female friends have sworn to never trust a man again. They now consider all men to be dogs or a means to get their bills paid. Some of my divorced male counterparts now look to women solely as objects of sexual gratification or as gold diggers trying to take them for every dime.

My purpose for writing this book is not to place blame, paint a picture of perfection or gain sympathy. I will not provide details that may shed a negative light on my ex-wife. I will however, share how the divorce affected me. I will impart spiritual and practical wisdoms that helped me transition from hurt to healing. This book is not only for my brothers and sisters in the Lord, but also for those who may not profess the Christian life. My prayer is that you will see the light of God's love in spite of what you have experienced.

Divorce doesn't have to be the end, but rather it can be a new beginning. Know that you still have so much to live for. As one who has endured the process of maturation, I encourage you to walk in confidence and hold your head high because your future promises to be great. And by all means, don't give up on love. You have heard the saying, "What doesn't kill you makes you stronger." After all I've been through; I can truly say that I have learned that trouble doesn't last always. There is indeed life after a painful divorce.

In His love,

Jonathan K. Sanders

L.A.P.D. - *Life After a Painful Divorce*

TABLE OF CONTENTS

CHAPTER 1

· · · · · · · · · · · · · · · · ·

Warning

The Signs before a Painful Divorce

The temperature in the house has changed. No welcome-home kisses to greet you. The cute little things your spouse has always done now aggravate you. Innocent requests escalate to intense arguments. Affirming words and compliments have transformed into accusations and assaults.

Conversations about bills and the children have replaced pillow talk. A virtual solid-steel wall has been erected in your bed or worse yet, you sleep in separate rooms. "Get out of my face," "I hate you," "I don't know why I ever married you," "My mother told me you were no good," becomes a part of everyday lingo. My, have things changed! You would have never thought in a million years that the look of love would have turned into the look of hate.

For some, the atmospheric pressure has such a dramatic change that recognizing the tornado-like climate shift is easy. While for others, the gradual ozone depletion goes unnoticed until the rising tsunami waters bring great floods and devastation. Each relationship and each person within the relationship is different. One disgruntled spouse may have his/her mate come home to a house void of family and furniture, while another may embody a landlord-to-tenant mentality and give a 30-day notice to vacate the premises. While you're out buying an offertory outfit to apologize for last night's argument, your mate is seated at the desk of a high-powered attorney.

Served and Being Served

Serving papers can be joyous or distressing depending upon where you stand in the process and if you are the server or the one being served. The experience can be like signing mortgage documents for your first home or like getting a letter from your doctor indicating that you have terminal cancer with only six months to live. If you were like me, wanting to stay married, this was a dreadful time.

How is it that a couple can have deep feelings for each other, but once the divorce is final, all that love is flushed down the toilet? The new behavior is like the waste treatment facility that churns the raw sewage. Did love ever abide in the union? I know we all have feelings and some of us act different than others but there definitely has to be a line drawn somewhere. I just believe no matter how angry or upset you are, there some things you just will not do. Slashing tires, busting windows, airing dirty laundry and sleeping with other people as a form of payback are just some of the lows. The depth of your relationship and integrity as a person can be measured by how you treat and respond to your soon-to-be ex. When you act out of your normal character, what you have done is given your soon-to-be ex power over you. Although you may feel like doing those things and may have a good reason, it's certainly best to refrain. If you're a man, always try to stay respectful, and if you're a woman, remain classy.

CHAPTER 2

. . . .

Issues with Divorce in the Church

Divorce is a sensitive topic and one of the most controversial subjects in the church. The topic of divorce has separated many Christians and has caused major arguments among religious leaders as a whole. Albeit common – the divorce rate among Christians exceeds the national average – few pastors delve into it. Some Christians believe that if you've been divorced, God will not forgive you. And remarriage? That takes a whole other spin on sin.

The Bible states that only one sin is exempt from His redemptive power.

> *Wherefore I say unto you, All manner of sin and blasphemy shall be forgiven unto men: but the blasphemy [against] the [Holy] Ghost shall not be forgiven unto men.*
>
> Matthew 12:31

Christians often misinterpret the following verse:

> *"For I hate divorce," says the Lord, the God of Israel, "and him who covers his garment with wrong," says the Lord of hosts. "So take heed to your spirit that you do not deal treacherously."*
>
> Malachi 2:16 NASB

Depending on the church and denomination, people do look at divorce differently. I personally believe that one can be divorced for a plethora of different reasons, including adultery, marrying someone addicted to drugs, marrying someone that is physically and/or emotionally abusive, or marrying someone that you did not know was gay. To look at a person who has been divorced and judge without knowing the reason is quite foolish.

On the contrary, who gets divorced seems to be more paramount than the divorce itself. For example, if you serve as an usher or musician in the church, you getting a divorce may not appear so bad because you are not in the forefront of the ministry. But if you serve in the forefront as a praise leader or the preacher, divorce can be preposterous. It's amazing who can get off the hook (so to speak) and who gets hanged by the neck. I've known people, who were not in the spotlight, divorce three and four times and no one bats an eye. On the other hand, if a person of prominence (who is seen and heard regularly on television and radio) gets a divorce, everyone wants to know the who, what, where, when and why.

Me being a preacher did not stop me from becoming a divorce statistic. Current data indicates that more than half of all marriages will end in divorce. Christian marriages have an even higher divorce rate estimated at almost 60 percent. Why? Because we go into marriages as broken vessels expecting our mates to fill the cracks and crevices. We don't prepare ourselves for oneness because many believe that being Christian is enough. Marriage has become less common for African-Americans. Even the U.S. Census reports that African-American households are the least likely to have a married couple in them compared to other ethnic groups. Yet it still indicates that we place a high value on marriage. Most churches do not provide effective marriage ministries to impart biblical and practical techniques nor create an environment to share in confidence without reprise or retaliation. So we hide marital strife to shun the shame and appearance of inadequacy. As for professional counseling…please! In certain communities, counseling is deemed an option only for the insane.

Some second marriages fail at approximately 60 percent due in part to spouses coming to the relationship with unresolved issues from the first marriage. The dynamics of stepfamilies when children – and yes, adult children – are involved has a major impact on second marriages. Following the trend, as the number of repeat marriages rise, the divorce rate climbs as well. Third marriages have a high incidence of divorce at almost 73 percent. African-Americans are significantly less likely than other racial/ethnic groups to ever marry, less likely to remarry, more likely to divorce, separate and cohabit and bear and rear children out-of-wedlock (and in mother-only households). Black women divorce at a rate nearly double of either white or Hispanic women. (*www.marriage101.org/divorce-rates-in-america, www.healthymarriageinfo.org*).

Some have even suggested that African-American couples divorce at a rate of 70 percent; second only to that of entertainers and professional athletes (65 percent).

Many saints believe that divorce is unforgivable in the eyes of God and the accused walk around as if they are forever tainted with a mark of sin. The accuser ignores the hurt and often inflicts more pain with insensitive comments.

The bottom line is that God is a forgiving God and He doesn't see like man sees. I, being a divorced preacher, would never judge without knowing the full facts and circumstances surrounding a person's divorce. Even then, I am nobody's judge. I met a preacher at the airport and in talking with him; he revealed that he has been married three times. At first, I looked at him like he must have some kind of problem only to find out in further conversation two of his wives died and his first wife left him for another woman. What about the woman who discovers her husband really likes men? Would you stay in a relationship like that? I'm sure you wouldn't expect someone to do what you are not willing to do, would you?

Can I Marry Again?

Many Christians believe that you cannot remarry once you have been divorced. Please know that the Bible doesn't say that, but man's traditions do. If your sins were forgiven by the grace of God, why would divorce be excluded? If a man can be forgiven of robbery or rape or if a woman can be forgiven for an abortion, then why can't you be forgiven for a failed marriage?

Of course you can remarry. Did God say that you can't or did a person interpret the bible the way they saw fit? You see, it's easy for a person on the outside looking in to tell you to stay in your marriage. As stated in Amos 3:3, "How can two walk together except they be agreed?"

I am not a proponent of divorce. I am not for divorce, but I am certainly for divorced people. If churches and organizations can have programs for former alcoholics and drug addicts, what about those that have been badly bruised by divorce and feel like their life is over? While I certainly prefer that couples fight to maintain the holy institution of marriage, I have learned the hard way that no matter how much you want a relationship to work, it will not survive if your spouse wants out of the marriage. You can be in a situation where one person doesn't want to change. A worse-case scenario is when a person marries you and then totally changes. They were so sweet, understanding, loving and caring until you said, "I do," and then they turned into a werewolf like it was a full moon. Everybody has the freedom of choice and not even God will bend you to obey Him. If that were the case, everyone would be saved and no one would be on drugs, alcohol or sinning period.

Church Criticism & Family Reaction

What are they going to say? How are they going to look at me? Am I a failure in their eyes? Will they think it's my fault? Am I still respected in the church or should I resign my position? I was really spazzing out! I was never the kind of person that really cared about public opinion but this was different. I counseled so many couples and kept their marriages together. I bragged about how wonderful my marriage was even when I really knew that it was on the rocks. I thought I was speaking faith but I was really ignoring the inevitable. When you're a leader, people never tend to think you are in trouble thus, you really get no help. I will admit that pride kept me from reaching out for a lifeline because a brother was sinking…and fast! Although you may never verbalize these types of questions, they will cross your mind.

Have you ever said, "I don't care what people think about me," but you knew deep down inside that it was an untrue statement? Even Jesus spoke out of concern for what people thought of Him.

> *When Jesus came into the coasts of Caesarea Philippi, He asked His disciples, saying, "Who do men say that I, the Son of Man, am?"*
>
> Matthew 16:13

Be honest. We all care, but on different levels. We care about the opinions of people who care about us. For those with whom we don't have much interaction, it doesn't matter that much. I thought for sure that churches that called me in for revivals, anniversary services, tent crusades and conferences would close their church doors on me and never invite me again. To my surprise, not one door closed and dozens more opened. I was shocked. This is a moment when I knew that God was on my side. The saying was coming to pass in my life that when you are down to nothing, God is up to something.

How Your Family Really Felt

The response from family can help or hinder your healing. A son needs to be reaffirmed by his mother, as does a daughter by her father. The validation renews confidence and develops a foundation for restoration. No woman wants to hear her father say, "You didn't treat him right. You should have cooked and cleaned instead of working overtime. You talk back too much. No wonder you're divorced. This mess is your fault!" Don't misunderstand me. Both spouses have a role in the demise of the marriage, but save the "constructive criticism" for later.

Being overwhelmed with failure is one thing, but the scolding of a parent can devastate a wounded soul beyond repair. Other than the leading of the Lord, they have been a voice of reason.

Want to know which of your siblings liked your spouse and who hated the fact that your mate consumed oxygen? The same sister who was a bridesmaid and smiled in your face on your wedding day may give you a piece of her mind before the dust settles on your divorce decree.

"I never liked him for you in the first place," "You could have done better than her," or "I probably should have told you this earlier, but while you were dating…" This purge of guilt is unfair to the newly divorced. To bombard a sibling with "could've, would've, should've" does nothing but further substantiate low self-esteem and bad judge of character. Why it is that it seems everyone becomes a psychic. It seems everyone else saw the pending doom and you missed it? The clairvoyant could have kept you from being a shriveled fragment of life in the corner.

Who Made You My Judge?

> *Judge not, that ye be not judged.*
>
> Matthew 7:1

Ah, the church: the place of refuge and strength; the house of healing and restoration; the advocate for openness and transparency.

The church: filled with judgmental, accusatory, faultfinding folks who charge you guilty and sentence you to life without the possibility of parole. The church: the breeding ground for hypocrites and haters; a place where people wear the mask of perfection and seventh-heaven holiness. I have come to find out that the church has condemned, convicted and gave people a life sentence with no parole with giving them a fair trial. Again every divorce is a different situation and you cannot judge until you hear the conclusion of the whole matter. Just think, you can be unjustly judging someone for getting out of a marriage that drove them crazy or caused them harm.

None of us are perfect, but striving to be perfected. As quiet as it's kept, we have all messed up and disappointed the Lord.

For all have sinned, and come short of the glory of God.

Romans 3:23

Many saints sing, preach, shout and worship with a bleeding heart because of divorce or other life crisis. How can the church accept and forgive drug use, fornication and homosexuality, yet shun those who have been divorced? It's the most hypocritical spirit operating in church today. Few ministries have programs that address needs specific to the divorced, albeit the largest growing population in the congregation. They have programs for children, youth, men and women; substance abuse programs; community outreach ministries; and more. But where do broken hearts go: the church, the psychiatrist or the nightclub?

Preaching Under Pressure

I have preached across the world and ministered to thousands while bleeding internally from hurt and failure. Here, I was leading while bleeding (literally). I didn't know how much time I needed to recuperate but I know I needed a break and bad! I felt like a doctor trying to give someone open heart surgery while he himself needed one. I have heard of preachers, especially pastors, taking a sabbatical for months and years, but my schedule wouldn't allow it. I would be in the airport with my ticket in hand heading to another revival saying to myself, "Man, just jump ship and go to Miami or Cali," but then I started thinking about Jonah and how the whale swallowed him up. A brother was not trying to cause the plane to crash (this is funny, but true). If it had not been for the Spirit of God, I don't see how I could have made it. Church leaders are expected to have power and experience, but those attributes come after tribulation.

I remember saying that I wished the churches would give me a break, but the calls doubled and sometimes tripled, and I didn't seem to have time to heal. I checked in and out of hotel rooms while thinking, "How can I help others when I can't help myself?" I didn't feel comfortable sharing with other preachers since they can also be judgmental.

I got up the nerve to talk to my dad who is also my pastor. I believed that maybe he would talk to me on a father and son level and give me strength to run on. I never went to him weak, but I was broken, which was difficult, because he never raised me that way. I never saw him have a weak moment and I'm sure he did, I just never saw it. Worse-case scenario I had hoped to receive spiritual solace from my father, but he simply said, "You're not the first and you certainly won't be the last."

"Wow," was all I could say. A brother can't get holy oil, laying on of hands or prophecy? I thought for sure we would have a long prayer and I would feel strengthened, but no! I was temporarily disappointed then, but when I look back at it now, I see he was merely pulling strength out of me I didn't know I had. I thank him every day of my life for not allowing me to sulk in my misery. I know so many people that have enablers around them who instead of help them, handicap them and think they are doing them a favor.

As an ex-marine, the phrase, "Only the strong survive," played in my mind. I used to sit in the church office before ministering wondering "how am I going to do this?" While the anointed praise and worship went forth in the sanctuary, the fear of failing the people, and more importantly God, tormented me. But by the time my hand touched the microphone, my spirit lifted and the scripture spoke to my heart.

And not only so, but we glory in tribulations also: knowing that tribulation worketh patience; and patience, experience; and experience, hope.

Romans 5:3-4

Not by might, nor by power, but by My Spirit, saith the Lord of hosts.

Zechariah 4:6

Once I realized that this situation was not about me and that I had people counting on me – my parents, children and peers – I was able to finish the task.

I commend my church family. They never treated me differently and I count that a blessing. Although at times, it appeared that some stood with baited breath to see if I would crumble under pressure.

"Bend, don't break."

CHAPTER 3

. . . .

Feelings

True Feelings Revealed

If you only learn one thing from this book, know that divorce hurts men too. Men have been trained to be tough and hardcore so we often suffer in silence. Although we appear strong, masked pain resonates deep inside. The first feeling that overtook me was failure. I used my parents' marriage as a measuring stick of marital success. My parents have been married for more than 45 years and I planned for my marriage to at least match their longevity.

It's a beautiful thing to go to a couple's home and see pictures of them dating several decades back. Naming your grandchildren and great-grandchildren is a privilege. Of course they've had troubles, but love is the glue that keeps them together. And though they don't look anything like they did years ago, their love has gotten stronger.

Failure told me, "You will never reach that goal so don't even try. Even if you do remarry, medical science only gives you about 71 years of life. By the time you meet, date and marry, you'll do good to see 20 years of marital strife – I mean bliss."

When I stood up to fear and resolved the dissolution of my goal, only then was I able to look in the mirror and admit that some things are not meant to be. We just don't know these things until it's too late, but yet isn't that a part of life? Just like all the money spent on the wedding dress, catering, flowers, rehearsal dinner and tuxedos, look at how much you could have saved, I told myself. I thought that life was over for me as the voice of failure continued to speak in my ear. However there was also another voice that I started to hear that became louder than the voice of failure – that voice was hope. As bad as I was feeling, I always held on to hope. Webster defines one meaning of hope as things will work out as God has planned. "Wow, I said to myself, sounds like Dr. Webster went to church that night!" (LOL) I felt optimistic that even though I was down to nothing, God was up to something. My life was not over, it just temporarily slowed down. I was getting ready and prepared for something that I had no idea was coming my way.

He'll put no more on you than you can bear were words I've heard all my life. Now these same words began to be food for my soul. Along with feeling sorry for myself, I looked in the mirror at the ripe age of 35 with no gray hairs, no missing teeth or pot belly; I shrugged my shoulders and told life, let's get it on. This wasn't going to be easy but I certainly was in it to win it. I didn't know how long it would take me to get through this, let alone get over it.

I once said that divorce is like being cut in half while still alive. The termination of a marriage has also been compared to ripping a sheet of paper and then trying to put it back together like new. Impossible! Jagged edges, small tears and unseen fragments do not allow for a simple paste or tape fix. Beyond the severance of ties, allocation of assets and establishment of visitation, insomnia, loss of appetite, mood swings and depression complicate the healing process. With that said, unless you've experienced the pains of divorce, you'll never fully understand its impact. The psychological pressure you feel going through a divorce is insurmountable. When you've lived, ate, slept, laughed and cried with someone for years, the two become one. What's even more crazy is that you can sometimes experience joy and pain at the same time. I know it sounds insane but I've known people who really wanted out of a marriage and when they finally get out, they wished they were back in. I don't know if it is simply because you've become adjusted to your mate or just social adaptation. Change is usually uncomfortable, even for the best of us.

Whatever your feelings are, let them be expressed and not suppressed. One of the worst things to see is an individual going through numerous emotional pressures, simply because they are not letting their feelings flow. In my experience, I've seen divorcees who curse, fight, argue and assault the other person, because they don't know how to deal with their feelings. A great sign of maturity and acceptance of what has happened is when one can control their feelings. This has been personally one of the greatest battles I faced through my ordeal. Most would not admit this, especially men. We act as though the greatest battles are external. But when it comes to divorce the battle is certainly internal.

Who's to Blame?

The who's-to-blame song will play in your mind until you decide to stop the music. Human nature seeks to find the source of the problem and more often than not, we start from the outside. It is easy to blame the ex for the demise of the relationship, however in doing so, your flaws go uncorrected. "It takes two to make a thing go right," and it also takes two to make a thing go wrong.

Even if the influence of a third party led to the divorce, the outcome inevitably falls upon the two spouses. The couple stood before God and man when they vowed to "forsake all others." I was in my mid-to late-30s at the time of my divorce. I believed that I was a well-versed, educated man. Through this process, I learned a lot about myself, my ex and my marriage. I have an intimate understanding of the statement, "You can learn as much from success as you can from failure."

Only a mature person can accept the part they played in the ruin of a marriage. Without introspection, ignoring your contribution will spew over, wreaking havoc into your next relationship and after several rounds of defeat, you may find yourself blaming everyone of the opposite sex. Look in the mirror and work through it. The process will not be easy, but what's the worst that can happen? You identify some shortcomings and then commit to improve and reinvent yourself.

Johari's Window[1] – created by Joseph Luft and Harry Ingham – helps individuals develop better relationships through improved interpersonal-communication skills. The window identifies four components – or panes – of awareness:

1. Things others know about me that I know (arena).

2. Things others know about me that I don't know (blind spot).

3. Things that others or I don't know about me (unknown).

4. Things I know about me that no one else knows (façade).

Create a checklist of pros and cons. Ask family and friends to describe you in four words: two positive and two not-so positive. Get a feel for who you are from the perspective of others. To get a true feel for their opinion, ask them to mail responses to you for anonymity. Tally the results and compare your adjectives with theirs.

Bad Habits Coming Back

Divorce can cause you to develop productive coping mechanisms or revert to bad habits. I know people who did a self-inventory, reinvented themselves and live a great life. I also have friends, both in and out of the church that turned to alcohol, drugs or sex in an effort to comfort the hurt.

When you are emotionally, mentally and financially spent, your defense is down. You become a vulnerable target open to anything that pacifies you. Destructive behaviors and bad habits that you conquered years ago may reappear seven times stronger. Smoking weed, drinking alcohol, going to nightclubs and sleeping around may come back like it never left. I didn't even mention the people that will help you self destruct because they think they are helping you and that you just need a little relief. But little do they know, some doors don't need to be opened again. You will find out that it's easy to start a fire, but hard as hell to put one out.

Divorce can deflate a man's self-esteem like a hot air balloon with a faulty burner. Getting a man to admit that is next to impossible, but believe me, it's true. You can hold a shotgun on him to confess this and most men rather you pull the trigger. Men internalize the rejection and use it to measure worth. The average man that has been divorced will never tell you that his wife left him. That will be too big a blow to his ego. He would rather lie and say she was a lesbian, on drugs, or even cheating on him to cover the truth. Now that's what you call a mess. It takes a real man to admit I ran her off, didn't give her the attention she needed, or wasn't the man I should have been. When he can do that, he is somebody that will have a great next relationship because he was honest with himself.

To boost the perceived worthlessness, many men turn to women. Once the word is out that a new bachelor is "on the market," opportunities are presented at the mall, church and work. What one woman tossed aside, many sisters are willing to pick up, dust off and take home. Sir, with your ego at zero, can you handle the temptation? Get to the place where you encourage yourself. Don't pacify; mortify the flesh.

> *So put to death the sinful, earthly things lurking within you. Have nothing to do with sexual sin, impurity, lust and shameful desires. Don't be greedy for the good things of this life, for that is idolatry.*
>
> Colossians 3:5 NLT

What about the wife who endured years of verbal abuse and left the marriage feeling ugly? Sure the new lipstick makes her feel a little better about herself, but it's the absence of negative energy that carries the real power.

Pygmalion effect2 is a means of asserting psychological control to influence a person's behavior. The tool can be used to ignite passion or diffuse aggression. If you repeatedly tell someone that they will never amount to anything, self-perception embodies those words and materializes in their actions. If you hear a lie enough times, you begin to believe it.

> *For as he thinketh in his heart, so [is] he Eat and drink, saith he to thee but his heart [is] not with thee.*
>
> Proverbs 23:7

Be careful
Be careful of your thoughts,
for your thoughts become your words.
Be careful of your words,
for your words become your actions.
Be careful of your actions,
for your actions become your habits.
Be careful of your habits,
for your habits become your character.
Be careful of your character,
for your character becomes your destiny.
—Author unknown

To fight off the psychological fiery darts of the enemy, master encouraging yourself. Look in the mirror, flash that great smile, say, "I have worth. I am attractive. I deserve the best God has for me." While you're flattering you, meditate on His Word.

> *And the Lord shall make thee the head, and not the tail; and thou shalt be above only, and thou shalt not be beneath; if that thou hearken unto the commandments of the Lord thy God, which I command thee this day, to observe and to do [them].*
>
> Deuteronomy 28:13

Life After a Painful Divorce

I have observed a divorcee jump into a new relationship with the ink still wet on the divorce decree. Don't be fooled into believing that a new companion is the solution. You must be totally healed and restored if you ever expect to have a fulfilled relationship. Otherwise, you'll be like a horse on a merry-go-round – going around in circles from one failed relationship to the next.

How Long Will I Feel Like This?

Experts have indicated that the grieving process takes a minimum of two years, but not necessarily in every case for everybody, especially not for me. That period allows the griever to experience holidays, birthdays and other memorable dates. Since divorce is a type of death, don't expect an overnight remedy. Please don't just jump back into dating and kicking it with people for the sake of not being by yourself. When you do this, you don't just bring baggage but luggage too. The healing process will take time and effort.

I encourage you to invest in your recovery: obtain the services of a professional counselor, start taking vacations, get into the best shape of your life and start reading books. Do something that refreshes you toward healing even if it takes a few years. I have seen my happiness radar jump from the bottom to the top. A part of true happiness in my opinion is looking back at where you have been and where you are now. It even garners greater strength for future battles knowing if you survived the former storms you will also the latter storms. When this is accomplished you will find yourself doing what I'm doing now and that's encouraging you, my friend. One of my greatest readings in the Bible was when Jesus tells the disciple Peter, when you come out of your storms and problems, reach back and strengthen someone else.

"Trouble don't last always" used to be an old saying to me, but now it's the living truth in my life. I thought I would always be sad, depressed, lonely and uncertain about my future. But now, I believe that my future is so bright, I'm going to need sunglasses! Hold on, my friend, weeping may endure for the night, but joy cometh in the morning!

CHAPTER 4

· · · · · · · · · · · · · · · · ·

What About the Children?

False Evidence Appearing Real

FEAR. False Evidence Appearing Real. Why do I feel like a failure, when I did not even want the divorce? Meeting after meeting with lawyers, real estate agents, family mediators and bank advisers wore on me, but nothing burdened me more than the custody battle for my sons. To have the fate of my children determined by a judge gripped me with fear.

I am a participatory father. I get involved and stay involved in my children's activities. In addition to instructing them on the ways of God, I help with homework, counsel them about women – as best as I can – and hang out with them. We ride bikes, play basketball and frequent the local game room. I still hold the title as "Air Hockey King."

I think that a father should spend quality time with his children. Guidance and impartation of wisdom doesn't happen by telepathy, and fulfilling financial obligations isn't enough to nurture responsible adults. Sadly, I didn't get a lot of time with my father. He preached around the world, ministered to thousands, but never attended one of my basketball games or tossed a ball in the yard. With eight children, it was understandable that he had to do what was necessary to support his family. I never held that against him, but I vowed to be active in my children's lives. He has certainly made up for that in the lives of my brothers and sisters. He showed us how to fix up our credit, buy cars and homes, and how to be productive citizens to society. I really love that about him, especially how he says in his sermons that he wished he had spent more time with his family instead of the church. When you look at it in the Bible, there was a family before a church. My dad has made up for so much in our lives, it is certainly commendable. He tells me all the time, "Son, spend time with your family because you can never get it back." I hold those words close to my heart and practice it every moment I get.

I have flown around the world and experienced numerous holding patterns due to inclement weather, arriving too soon or problems on the ground. The delay ripples into more delays, missed connecting flights and frustrated passengers who have no control over the situation. Waiting for the outcome of the divorce proceedings put my life into a holding pattern and consumed my every thought. My life came to a dead stop. I could not function. I could not focus. What if the magistrate decides that my boys will get better care from their mother? When will I get to see them? How will that affect our relationship? I had to draw upon the sermons that I preached to encourage others, for my own peace of mind.

"No matter what you're going through, God has your back. He promised that He'd never leave or forsake you, so stand in the midst of your storm, grab your anchor and hold on. He's got you covered."

Even the Scripture on my business cards boasted about my faith in Him.

> *What shall we then say to these things? If God be for us,*
> *who can be against us?*
>
> Romans 8:31

After months of waiting, I tried to reason with God and call in a favor.

"Lord, You are the potter and I am the clay. You are the blacksmith and I am the precious metal. You are the creator and I am the creation. I know that You have my best interest at heart, but Lord, this one is too much. I can't take anymore. I have done what You asked and I need You to come through for me right now."

Well, the Lord called my bluff. Not being able to go one more day, turned into holding on a few more weeks and then months. He knew that I would not walk out on my children or Him, and more importantly, He knew that I needed a little more time in the purifying fire.

Through that agonizing wait, I learned that when I felt most alone, God was working it out for my good. Like the air traffic controller, He saw things that I couldn't. Despite the minor inconvenience, He steered me clear of turbulence and taught me how to trust Him in the midst of turmoil.

Unless the Lord had been my help, my soul had almost dwelt in silence when I said my foot slippeth, Thy mercy, oh Lord, held me up.

Psalm 94:17-18

How did it turn out? Keep turning the pages, you'll see.

Children Caught in the Shuffle

I have never experienced the pain of a severed limb, but a severed heart, excruciating. The worst feeling I have endured was to see the pain in my children's eyes. Unlike a drowning child, my boys never cried out for help but I read their eyes: hurt, fear, and confusion. The pain pierced deep, so I asked my wife to prolong filing the divorce.

She emphatically said, "No! I want out! Just tell the boys that we both want this."

"That's a lie." I argued. "I don't want this divorce, you do!" My head and heart were open to work on the marriage and I knew God's stance on it.

Initially, I refused to let go. In doing so, I said within myself, I'm going to hold you against your will and make you be with me. In some states, that's kidnapping. Love should captivate, not capture. Let's say that your car has been hijacked by an armed assailant. You drive your fingernails into the rear bumper unwilling to let this jerk speed away with what you worked so hard to obtain. He careens down an alley at 60 miles-per-hour dragging you through potholes and broken bottles. What began as a refusal to give up your car now jeopardizes your life. Let go, file a claim with your insurance company and get another car.

When you let go, you save yourself unnecessary pain and heartache. Don't disrespect yourself or God by thinking that because this person left you, your life is over. God didn't design you to stalk them by driving past their house at night to see whose car is in the driveway or by their job at lunch to see who they're going out with. Don't stoop low and start spying through binoculars or calling 20 times an hour from a blocked number. In letting go, you open yourself to the positive energy that can connect you with someone better. Love can be better the second time around.

I've heard horror stories about children of divorced parents who went buck wild. To numb the pain or in a desperate attempt for attention, they delve into sex, drugs, truancy, and even suicide. I had invested much time and love into developing my boys into men, yet I feared the worst.

Refusing to lie to my boys, I stated my objection to the divorce on numerous occasions, which led to many arguments. When the divorce was inevitable, I had a heart-to-heart talk with my boys who were then 10 and 11 years old.

I explained that their mother and I loved them. In an effort to minimize their guilt, I reiterated that the divorce was not their fault. I compelled them to not harbor resentment against either of us. "Your mother is not a bad person; however, she believes that this choice is in her best interest."

A major factor in their resilience was that my wife and I both loved them through the transition. We committed to spending quality time with them. We reassured them of our love both in word and deed.

It's All About the Children, Right?

"Your request for joint custody will be denied." The agonizing words of her attorney reverberated through me. Once the shock wave subsided, anguish settled. What was her motive for denying me equal time with my boys? I have witnessed the chaos caused on so many children – especially boys – whose fathers were absent.

"Satan, not my boys!"

Up to that point, I had been somewhat cool, accommodating and amicable, but when the furnace was ignited, I turned up the heat. I showed up hostile at my attorney's office for an unscheduled meeting.

"Whatever it takes to make this happen, make it happen. I am not a child-support-pay-check daddy. I'm a quality-time daddy." I placed a wad of money on his desk. "I'm ready for the fight of my life. They need me in their lives and I need them in mine."

My attorney said, "Jonathan, it can get very expensive. You will have to hire a private lawyer to represent them solely. They may even have to take the stand in court and state where they want to live."

I encouraged my sons to be honest with the magistrate. I refused to put undue pressure on them and expressed that I supported whatever decision they made.

"We want to be with both you and Mommy."

When their mother heard what they were going to say, she backed down. The boys did not have to endure questioning and I won guardianship as the custodial parent. Hallelujah!

A Change of Religion

I breathed relief and celebrated for eight minutes and then my ex-wife told the boys that she had changed religion and was a member of the Nation of Islam. After being a Christian for 13 years and accepting her calling as a minister, she migrated to the Muslim faith. For a brief moment, I wondered if she was ever saved. But seeing as how I am a ways off from perfection, I decided not to be judgmental, but I felt betrayed. Here I was gifted with the ability to discern people in different congregations in my travels across the world. I could look at a person for two seconds and can pick up exactly what was going on in their life, yet I couldn't discern what was going on with my own wife. I was so depressed when she gave me this news, wondering where I went wrong. Was I a hypocrite? Did I let God down and make one of his daughters leave the kingdom?

When the boys returned from a visit with their mother, they told me that they were no longer allowed to eat pork. She told them that swine was not good for them and she would not be buying or preparing it. I don't mind a little pork on my fork, so that rule didn't transfer to my house.

The boys bombarded me with questions about this new religion. They grew up in Christianity and the contradicting values and beliefs confused them – and me. How can you walk with God faithfully for 13 years and then change gods because of divorce? What did Jesus do to turn her away from Him?

As clearly as the words are printed on this page, God spoke to me. He told me that I must not fuss or argue with her, but simply pray for the sister.

"Sir, yes Sir!"

CHAPTER 5

. . . .

Money, Money, Money...MONEY!

How will I pay my bills? Will I lose my car, house, everything I have accumulated during the marriage?

On the surface, two incomes should equal more money, but that may not always be the case. Possibly due to a lack of trust or the inability to relinquish control, many couples do not combine incomes. I know couples who have never seen each other's pay stub. Amazing!

You can make it with one or two incomes. It's all about how you have handled your finances throughout your entire life, not just while you were married. That's why some people who have never been married still own a home, car or business. God has destined you to be blessed. That blessing is not connected to a marriage contract.

Being divorced may cost you lots of money. When you are on the financial rebound and have finally landed on your feet, your money mentality will greatly improve. I cried on how much my divorced cost me, but I dried my eyes quickly because I had a father who taught me from a young age how to handle money and not let money handle me. He pushed me to get my first job as a grocery-store bagger at 12. At 15 years old, I worked at McDonald's. When I showed him my first check – expecting a handshake, full smile and congratulations – he deducted $50 and called it my monthly rent payment. What in the world? A teenager with a mortgage? My nostrils flared and sweat beaded on my forehead. I knew better than to verbally challenge my father, but I couldn't control the nonverbal rage. Today, I realize that he taught me principles of financial stewardship that will benefit me throughout life.

I compel anyone coming out of divorce to stand on your own feet. Don't run to your parents or friends who will try to rescue you. Walk the burning embers of financial restoration, bring forth pure fruit and take pride in your accomplishment. If you have to leave a four-bedroom home with a two-car garage, then start with a one-bedroom apartment in the hood, at least your name will be on the lease. I see people who keep company with others that will feed into their needs instead of pushing them to take the long, but sure way.

I will admit that when I first got divorced, I was caught up in buying things to mask my pain such as clothes, lavish vacations, expensive restaurants, jewelry and the like. I never realized how buying is connected to how you feel inside. I noticed that when I bought things, I would say this is going to help me get over the divorce. How silly was I? What does a white-gold diamond ring or a $500 suit have to do with your inner mental healing? Not a thing. So many of my peers have been operating on this level for years and are still without financial maturity. They have 20 pairs of gators, three or four cars with high payments, $25,000 in jewelry and clothes like a department store, all to mask how they really feel inside. Happiness is not having what you want but wanting what you have.

> *But my God shall supply all your need according to*
> *His riches in glory by Christ Jesus.*
>
> Philippians 4:19

If you want to get to the heart of a person's character, see how they act when it comes to money – in abundance and lack. I have heard of divorcing couples who have fabricated untruths to get over financially. The worst is when a man dodges the responsibility of caring for his children.

Is it true that women get the bigger piece of the pie financially or is it simply a myth? Should one get more than the other solely based on gender? Of course men say, "No." Almost every woman I know says, "Yes," despite the fact that many women make comparable salaries with respect to men. Or should the most money go to the one who got the short end of the stick. For example, the man who runs off with his mistress and leaves his family, or the woman who skips town with her boss. Why should one be rewarded with the fruits of marriage – house, car, spousal support – when they cut down the family tree? Sometimes, even our court system doesn't get it right and give a harvest to someone who has not sowed. In the long run, fate will run its course and things like this always find a way to work themselves out.

I've seen cases where the man had an affair and divorced his wife for his mistress, hid his assets and money only to have his mistress leave him for somebody else in the next few years. I've heard of women who were married, cheated, and got pregnant by somebody else, then still took their husbands to the cleaners financially and broke his heart only to find themselves in a few short years with no man, no child support and living on the welfare system. What am I saying you ask? God don't like ugly and what comes around goes around. You can't get over by taking somebody else under, period.

Should You Benefit from the Divorce If You Caused It?

I applaud individuals who bow out gracefully because of indiscretions. Some men know they messed up, slept around and were physically abusive. But the sign of a bad man gone good is when he decides to release his wife – without a fight – because he's unable to remain faithful, cannot stop the abuse or realized that he's not the marrying type. Some women abandon their family for a new man who can "put it down," yet still want spousal support, the car and the kitchen sink. Is the best reality a good lawyer or placing it in God's hand? Both. Don't be a fool and don't be super spiritual.

When I learned how much I had to pay to settle my divorce, I felt like I had been punched in the throat by a heavy weight champion: speechless, breathless, dazed and confused. I wanted to stay in our house, while my ex wife wanted to sell it. The disparity tortured me. I loved our home. The neighborhood, with its mature trees, manicured landscapes and filled with the laughter of children, reminded me of a sunny California town. I knew most of the neighbors by first name and it was in walking distance from the kids' elementary school. Tears welled in my eyes when the real estate agent put the "For Sale" sign in the front yard.

As I worked on the lawn or washed my car, my neighbors inquired, "Where are you moving to?" Embarrassed, I tactfully found a way to change the subject.

Oh, but thank God for legal representation with the experiential foresight to see what I could not. My lawyer advised that to maintain stability for the children, I should buy my wife out and stay in the home. I agreed. As a result, it minimized disruption to my boys' routine by introducing them to only one new environment – their mother's residence.

But right after that, I was faced with child support, which would have been no problem because I was raised by a father, who told me to always take care of your kids. But when the arguments came and I was told, "I'll do whatever I want with your money," I sought advice from my lawyer. I knew I wanted joint custody anyway because I could never deal with just getting my boys on the weekends. That was when I was told by my lawyer that I needed to pursue joint custody. That would give me a total of two weeks a month with my boys. I prayed to God because I love my kids and this option would be the ultimate blessing. I even fasted the day of court for favor with the magistrate. My prayers were answered. Not only was joint custody awarded, I was named the custodial parent: the boys' primary home was at my residence. I danced so much that I could have taken James Brown's crown. Despite a system that often labels men as "deadbeat dads who don't care about their children," God favored my petition.

The boys expressed excitement too. They had love for both parents and did not want to solely be at either parent's house. I tell my fellow brethren that kids are often placed with their mothers because most fathers do not fight for custody. According to the National Center for Health Statistics, the courts side with women 90 percent of the time in custody battles. In my opinion, custody battles seem to be hardest on African-American fathers, probably because of the combination of gender and racial discrimination. But thank God men are waking up, forming organizations like the Fatherhood Educational Institute and the website DadsRights.com. Men, take your rightful place. Let us let the world see that good black fathers exist.

The situation gets much stickier when you enter a relationship and your new companion doesn't want your kids around. I know too many examples to name. I'm shocked how someone can choose a lover or spouse over their own children. I've even known some men to move in with a woman who has kids but his kids are not welcomed. Ridiculous! Just imagine how the children feel? Sometimes, it's best to wait if you have small children instead of forcing someone on your kids. In some of my counseling sessions as a minister, children issues are one of the main reasons couple's divorce. Clashes erupt between your kids and their kids. Most children want to see their biological parents together, but when they mature, they understand differently. I've personally watched my sons change throughout the past few years. At first, they never said anything about a woman, but as teenagers, they often ask, "Where are the ladies, Dad?" It's quite amusing now that I think about it. Don't be so hard up for companionship that it will destroy the trunk of the family tree.

When I look back at it now, as much as I love my kids I wish I hadn't stayed in a messed up marriage as long I did.

A New Type of Woman

I'm excited to know the pendulum has swung in the favor of the women. They have imported cars, their own house, money, ministry and their own businesses. Hey, we even had a woman presidential candidate on the ballot. Female pastors, sheriffs, mayors and the list continues. A new type of woman is on the forefront and this brings great excitement to real men who are not inferior. The new type of woman that I'm seeing is an absolute breath of fresh air to society. However where there's the new, the old is still somewhere hanging around. Despite this fast trend that's sweeping across the world, there are still some women who have the old mentality that they can only receive and never give. It's not unusual for a woman to ask the man out, and pay for the movie and dinner. This may sound contrary to some women but if you ask him out, shouldn't you cover the cost? Women that receive and do not give back into the relationship nothing but time and conversation will find it hard to get a good man. Although God created men to be givers and women receivers, can't a brother get a home-cooked meal, a card or a gift just to know he's special and appreciated?

It's a major turnoff when I meet a woman who off the back carries the aroma of being a taker. This is why I believe so many men at times are apprehensive about certain relationships. Some men will spoil you to death: fly you around the country on an all-inclusive trip, buy you jewelry and clothes and support your children financially in the absence of their dead-beat daddy. One of my brothers (I have four, so stop guessing) took a young lady out on a date, and before dinner was over, she asked if she could order food to go for her children. He was cool with it and said okay. For their next three dates, she repeated her take-home order. On the fourth date, he told her that her actions were crass. And would you believe she had the nerve to get an attitude? Needless to say, the dating ceased.

A woman with a 720 FICO score is far more attractive to me than long hair and French-tip nails. The hair may be weaved, the tips fake, but a good credit rating cannot be counterfeited. We brothers don't mind bringing the table and chairs, but help us put something on it. When I see a sister who has her own, it is one of the most elegant things I've ever seen. So many women use the excuse for where they are by saying that they don't have a man, they have kids and no child support or bad credit is the culprit. Yet these same women are the ones spending all their money on hair care products, clothes and going out to eat three times a week with their girlfriends. So tell me who's to blame for where they are in their lives?

Competition is high among women, which has caused many to wear their wealth on their backs. And despite the insurmountable bills that keep piling up, they go to church, hucking and bucking, breaking fingernails, losing ponytails and saying, "Lord, make a way." He made a way with an income-earning job, but many have cursed themselves with bad decisions, which eventually become bad habits.

CHAPTER 6

. . . .

Social Separation

Divorce can make you retreat from or advance toward socialization. You may avoid certain people or groups you once cherished while clinging to new – seemingly incompatible – folks. The shift is a matter of trust. Weddings and funerals bring out the real person. I'm adding divorce to that list.

There were times when I was home bored to death because it was a time I'd be spending time with my sons but this wasn't my weekend. When I looked around my half empty house cold and quiet, I felt tears well up in my eyes. Refusing to succumb to depression that was loudly banging on the door of my soul, I found another hobby. After spotting it in a local newspaper, I went to the pistol range. I fired guns back in the day when I was in the U.S. Marine Corps so this brought back old feelings. My buddies and I had a blast at the range and I left feeling like "Dirty Harry."

Mob Mentality

Some people will step back from you as if you had a deep, raspy cough during a flu pandemic and you didn't bother to cover your mouth. These spectators stand on the sidelines waiting to see the outcome of the game: will you fold under the pressure or will you come out on top?
While some run away from you, a plethora of others run toward you. They come bringing gifts of unsolicited advice, invitations to pity parties and a list of unmarried friends looking to get hitched. You didn't ask for a cheerleading squad when an occasional, "Are you okay?" would suffice.

My Mood is Different

The bombardment of negativity from the ex—or others in disbelief of the divorce—can lead to self-induced isolation. It's easier to mope alone than the continuous recitation of the gory details. On the other hand, introspection can reveal things about yourself that you would rather not believe, so you seek solace from strangers for validation. Misery loves company.

Environment is Everything

To maneuver through the alternating moods, I learned the power of navigation. Navigation is influence. Either you influence your environment or it influences you.

I grew up in the projects of Harlem with gangs, guns and prostitution. A standard fixture in the community was a plastered heroin user slumped in the gutter. I didn't know good neighborhoods existed. Even the ones on TV were like something out of a fairy tale. But as my dad's ministry grew we moved to Jamaica, Queens. The ten of us—Mom, Dad, five boys, three girls—lived in a house rather than a three-bedroom apartment. I thought the garage in the back was somebody else's house! It was almost too real to believe that this house was now our home. From the pit to the palace. Hallelujah!

Stay away from people who try to keep your conversation in the past. If you dwell on the past, that's where you'll stay. Remember: we walk where we watch, so look to your future.

Creating New Surroundings

I challenge you to create a powerful environment which breeds success. Cleave to those who push you to your future. Find people who will support, encourage and challenge you. Once you've created your amen corner, take caution not to zap their energy with pathetic groveling. Don't use the divorce as an excuse for helplessness. No one wants to be around an adult who acts like a spoiled child—divorced or not. Don't take your supporters for granted. Express appreciation often.

When you see a person who is calm in the midst of a tumultuous storm, you witness someone who has adapted to the situation. If you live in an efficiency apartment, work a minimum-wage job but you're working toward homeownership, then surround yourself with people who have "arrived" where you're trying to get. If you want to be a millionaire, spend time with millionaires. If you want to be a doctor, network with doctors. If you want a home and financial stability…You get the point.

No one chooses your friends but you. Even God grants you liberty to pick your pals. Choice is a powerful privilege, use it wisely. Survey your relationship environment. Does it stimulate or suffocate you? If it's the latter, run!

A psychologist friend of mine said, "Show me your friends and I'll show you your future." If you have a negative environment absent of hope, darkness fills the future and you are in trouble. I make a conscious effort to have minimal interaction with bitter divorced people and the unhappily married. Try as you might, the conversation will migrate to, "there is no such thing as a happy marriage" and "life is over after divorce." The truth of the matter is their situation does not have to be yours. If you allow their awful experience to ferment in your mind, a bag of what-ifs will filter into future relationships.

— What if shes acting nice until I marry her?
— What if hes only after my body?
— What if the interest is in what I have, not who I am?

We may never know the truth, but God does. A committed relationship with your heavenly Father can help you stay focused on His will and not your own. Just as a close friend has your back, He has a way of warning you of pending danger. Will you listen or will that woman's beauty or that man's physique drown out His voice?

CHAPTER 7

. . . .

The Other Sex: I'll Never See Women the Same

After the divorce, I looked at women differently. My experience with one woman angered me so much that it clouded my perspective toward other women (excluding my mother. She's the sweetest woman in the world. Don't laugh, that's my mother.) Self-centered, manipulative and needy became my opinion. Regardless of how kind, intelligent, spiritual and beautiful, I perceived they had impure motives. Despite my twisted thinking, I tried not to disrespect or mistreat any woman. I ain't crazy. My mother wouldn't have it.

I opted for a disconnected connection with women. I gave them just enough of me to show interest but distanced myself emotionally. It only took a couple of outings for the façade to be revealed. Women looked at me like they had hit the chocolate lottery. Even though I told them I was not ready for a relationship, they insisted I would change my mind once I got to know them.

I learned that some men resort to nonproductive means. Some promise a lasting relationship knowing she is nothing more than a booty call. Others take deliberate steps to demoralize women as a form of payback to the ex-wife. What shocked me more than the antics of men were the antics of women – desperate for the attention – they allowed it.

Tell me if any of these things sound familiar:

— Picking up the tab on a date that he initiated
— Running his errands
— Washing his clothes

— No public displays of affection (if you even go out together)
— Spending quality time, but only after midnight (And you know that means you're just a booty call)

This type of woman believes that if she keeps doing everything he wants, he will eventually become her man. That lie has to be the biggest one this side of the Mississippi River. Ladies, stop it! Love yourself more than you love being in a relationship.

My advice: be considerate and forthright. If you intend to remain unattached and date several people, let each one of them know. I withdrew when the conversations were getting too serious about the future which eventually led to arguments. I recognized my actions as a flaw in character and sought help. I went to the library to investigate and realized it was a natural trait to at times not want a fully committed relationship. In other words there are some people that all they want is dinner and a movie and nothing else! The challenge is to be able to accept that or simply move on.

I have never met a man who was attracted to a woman he can treat like a doormat. His boo? Of course because she is at least feeding his ego and making him feel like he can have his way. Don't let men fool you, we love it. But when a man is picking a wife for life, or the queen of his dreams, he wants a woman who has a little backbone (just not bigger than his backbone). And there you have it. Man's best-kept secret: a soft sweet woman yet not just a total pushover. What makes a man know he has the right one is when he thinks he has all the answers but she shows him through her femininity that her answer is sometimes much better!

I have heard elderly women say that a man is no match for a woman. After being out of the dating circle for more than a decade, I learned that the "sistahs" had enough game to play in the NFL. Scandalous, manipulative and self-centered. At this quarter in life, I am less tolerant of foolishness. I am not labeling all women. I know women who embody the essence of virtue spoken of in Proverbs 31.

While women can be the sweetest, kindest, most loving creations of God, others deserve an Oscar for the stellar performance of imitating a virtuous woman.

As I've said before, "Finding a good wife in a time like today is like finding a glass of ice water on the south side of hell." Some women only look for men who have an influential or prestigious position such as a doctor, preacher, lawyer or any status that keeps her in the limelight. God help it if she is only physically attracted without a desire for emotional connection. Flawless skin, enticing eyes, well-groomed with broad shoulders; none of these characteristics make the man. He can have all the looks yet be lazy, abusive and disrespectful and even on the down low. You want him because he looks good and you look good with him? I think not.

Where There is Admire, There is Desire

Being divorced I see things totally different than I did when I was married. There is so much that is obvious to me that I was oblivious to when I was married. Women's motives are so apparent to me. Now don't let me throw you by that statement because there are a lot of decent women. But at the same time there are some that have the wrong motives or ulterior motives to say the least. You have many good women that will wait until it's their time for a man in their lives, but you also have those that will make it happen by any means necessary. Mom said to me "Son, always remember the average woman is at least three steps ahead of you in the game of love!" Lawd was she so right!

Some women are consumed with the title "girlfriend" or "wife." The moniker makes them feel whole, but they lose sight of the purpose of the relationship. I witnessed a woman manipulate a public display of affection – grabbing her man's hand – to mark her territory. She smiled, accentuated her sway and put him on display like he was a gold medal at the Olympics. When a man feels like he's been conquered like a city overthrown in a war, he will revolt.

When I'm courting a woman I can't help but to ask myself, "Why am I here?" Is my role to wash her car, take out her trash, pay her bills, or get her hair and nails done? In my experience, many women have the mentality that men should do all that and more. Let me clarify; I do not have a problem doing things for women, however reciprocity is critical in a relationship. If all she brings is long hair and stunning looks, I'm good. Chivalry is not dead, but no man wants to feel used.

A needy woman who gives nothing to sustain the relationship will run a man away. Since women can earn just as much money as men, doing a little something for a man on occasion does not detract her femininity. I don't care what nobody says, you can have all the love in the world, but dating somebody with bad money habits (phone disconnected, car repossessed, moving from place to place, and borrowing money from family and friends) will never be in style. When a man has a woman who will pick up the tab if he's low on funds, he has a jewel.

Women act differently when I'm in my Mercedes versus my '1992 Toyota Camry. Guess which car I'm driving based on the following scenarios:

— The blinkers are flashing, I'm gesturing turn signals out the window, trying to make eye contact and women wont let me change lanes.
— Women smile, wave and call out to me.

A gold-digger is like a silent cancer and what's worse is that the church can be filled with them. Men are not looking for a wife in the church but rather in the kingdom. A church woman seeks a prophecy saying she will marry a husband who will pay her bills, while a kingdom woman understands the ways of a virtuous woman, meaning don't wait for a man but work your hand until the man comes. She can manage her household and be a help to her husband. Kingdom women don't wait on a knight in shining armor – Armani custom-tailored suit – and white horse –a Mercedes S-Class – to rescue them from the dungeon of life. Kingdom women are employed homeowners who may have a business. Church women have the appearance of virtue as they jump and shout, dance and scream, but refuse to save for a home or get educated on investing. Then, they wonder why a brother from church dates a woman he met at the supermarket rather than a sister on the praise team. Now before you turn me off obviously I'm not talking about every woman. There are some church women that don't have this attitude and there are some kingdom women who are not home owners. In so saying, there's nothing wrong with meeting a woman who goes to church but have a kingdom mentality and you meet her at the mall! Don't be damsels in financial distress; position yourself to receive His blessing.

Sex is the Last Resort for a Companion

Is sex overrated? You better believe it. Sex should be one of the last reasons for companionship. This may not seem necessary to mention to you, but in a world filled with sexism this is a very important question. I've been told that in relationships between one to ten good sex is a 7 for women and a 9 for men! I asked a question a while back on my blog program that went like this: In a moment of weakness if you had sex with your fiancé and found the sex to be horrible would you still marry them? The majority said "no" for various reasons. I wonder why that is? Is it because sex is so overrated in relationships? Now that's the raw truth to many people that will be honest. But at the end of the day is that all you want out of your mate? I know I don't. You can have a man who has bedroom skills that take you to the moon and back. But if he can't hold a steady job or is abusive – verbally or physically – is the great sex really worth it? Girlfriend may have the ability to drop it like it's hot and cause your pinky toes to curl up toward the heavens, but will her sex skills cause you to ignore her 16-year-old mentality? Doubtful.

Society has put sex and sexism at the top of the list. Music videos, tight jeans and low-cut blouses are a part of life. I know women who have said that they won't even talk to a man with small feet and hands. Stop laughing. I'm telling the truth. Now what if that small-footed brother made $150,000 a year and owned a string of apartment complexes? That would make his feet more attractive than those of a seven-foot tall NBA star. Men are just as bad. If she isn't packing in the back, she doesn't get the time of day, but if she's built like a brick house, she can write her own check – or get him to write it.

If that same brick house of a woman has annihilated credit, lives with three kids at her mother's home, unemployed but gets her hair and nails done weekly, and has a stank attitude, are you still interested? Probably not.

Balance is best because that figure-eight body may one day be a zero. I did not always have this mind set, but at 42, my thinking has matured. Good sex doesn't make a man commit, but a good woman does. By all means, don't get married because the sex is good, but rather, because the relationship is good. If you're connected only because of sex, you will soon become bored with each other. I love fried chicken, but every day, all day? Can someone say salmon, please?

Some women will go to great lengths to improve bedroom skills, but never consider enhancing the total package. I have never heard my friends say, "I'm going to marry that woman. She has the best stuff I've ever had." The list of attributes below – not in any particular order – describe the idea of an attractive woman:

— high morals
— cleanliness
— good-paying job
— good credit
— car
— education
— respectable children

No one knows what you like as much as you do. By all means, if you like dark men, go for what you know. If you've always been attracted to light-skinned women, do you. Don't let anyone make you feel bad about your preferences. Parents and pastors sometimes make a drastic mistake in this aspect. They often have good insight, but in the final analysis, you have to be attracted to the physical, spiritual, emotional and intellectual character of that individual.

Remarriage

I wouldn't consider marriage with any woman without first seeing these four records:

1. Criminal. These days, who you see is not who you get. You can view someone's criminal record for free or for a few pennies on the Internet. You can be dating the check-fraud queen and not even know it. He can be a dope dealer with a rap sheet as long as your arm, but his warm smile and endless gifts have blinded you. And to single women with daughters, how horrified would you be to learn that your man is a pedophile two years into molesting your daughter? It would take all day to tell you about people who thought they were dating Dr. Jekyll, but all along he was Mr. Hyde. Anyone who objects to you seeing their criminal record…you eject!

2. Medical. Have you thought about being married to a sick person, with high blood pressure, diabetes or worse – some incurable sexual disease? She may be barren and you want a child. Or a man who can't (Lord, help me) get it up because of his blood pressure. "Houston, we have a problem!" This matter may seem dismal, but if you become the primary caregiver to your mate, you will realize the importance. From sleepwalking to chronic insomnia, you should be privy to the health of your future mate.

3. Driving record. Road rage, drunk driving or a tendency to run stop signs are negative aspects to a person's personality. If you're the one who's in the car, then all of that matters. As a passenger on dates, I have felt like I wouldn't make it out of the car alive. I have a

female friend who went on a date, and by the time they arrived at the movie theatre, she got out of the car crying and shaking screaming, "Never again." With the high incidences of car crashes, your companion's driving record is essential. A poor driving history can double your premium, when added to your insurance policy. I know married couples who have had to get separate policies for that exact reason. By all means, know what you're getting into, before you get into that car.

4. Credit Report. The Bible says that the wicked borrow and do not repay – paraphrased from Psalm 37:21. When you are with a dishonest person, life can be challenging. It is one thing to have a situation that has a negative impact on your credit, but it's another thing when derogatory credit is characteristic of your financial decisions. Connecting with an individual with a shady financial past will create long-term problems in a relationship. Who wants to deal with late payments, screening calls for creditors or hiding the car in your cousin's garage to avoid the repo man? Let me clarify that bad credit doesn't make the person bad. Many good people have made financial mistakes out of ignorance, immaturity or impulse. It is awesome to see an individual repairing their credit with payments to their creditors, downsizing to a more affordable home or changing vehicles to better manage the payment. If you're 40, vacationing and splurging on shopping sprees with a pile of bills on your kitchen table, that's ludicrous. Trust me when I tell you… romance with bad finance is a nuisance.

CHAPTER 8

. . . .

Rated R: Sex and the Newly Single Man

As a single man, the opportunities for a woman, wife or boo are limitless. At last count, I estimated ten women to every man. Taking into consideration the number of men on drugs, unemployed, incarcerated or with a propensity or fondness of other men, a "good" man is a rare find. Some men use this uniqueness to their advantage at the expense of women's self-esteem.

When I first divorced, I dated as often as possible out of boredom, loneliness and to see if a brother still had it to be honest. All sizes, shapes and educational backgrounds were accessible to me. I saw more of my city in those few years – movie theatres, jazz lounges, ice cream parlors and restaurants – than I did in the 13 years I was married. Like Ricky Martin sang, a brother was living la vida loca! LOL.

I believed that the plethora of women would soothe my sore heart. I convinced myself that although my wife didn't want to be bothered with me, these women did.

When the benevolent women heard my story and empathized with my pain, they gave me all they had to offer. My boys and I ate like celebrities with a different gourmet chef preparing each meal. Offers for clothes, cash and unmentionables soon followed. I did an occasional chest check to make sure that a bull's eye hadn't been plastered on me. Beyond assertive to aggressive – an unfamiliar territory for a pursuer like myself. I didn't expect the cat to chase the dog. What in the world? Beautiful women with fascinating careers, homes, cars – the total package – in hot pursuit of me.

Sexual frustrations will run high for the average divorcee. You go from getting it on the regular to not at all. It will take much wisdom to make it in the sex-crazed society we live in today. Hardly anybody is wearing clothes and when they do, you still see their undergarments. Sex today in the dating circle has become as common as a shaking of the hand. So much attention has been given to it and you are now judged by not what kind of person you are but by your bedroom skills. If you're a woman, most brothers that can't sleep with you in the first 30 days tend to move on. If you're a man and don't try to hit in 30 days they say your gay. What in the world? I hate to say this but very few people can date without, at one time or another, engaging in a sexual relationship with their mate. I personally know of only a few people that can remain abstinent (even some that are married). A hard saying, but true.

Dealing with the advances from women is always an awkward moment. In our culture now, it's not strange for a sister to step to a brother hard…making her intentions crystal clear. When I was married, it was bad but nowhere near to what it is now. Aggression is not bad in its place, but when a woman makes it appear she's desperate, she will definitely attract the wrong man. When I first got divorced, I didn't care for these advancements because my heart was broken. Needless to say, some women took it personally and cursed me out for thinking I was all that. LOL. I didn't fault them because they couldn't see my heart, but boy was that a trip. Men see the advances from women as flattery, but personally, I'd rather be the aggressor. One of the worst is when a married woman steps to me. I know that marriage is challenging, but if it's that bad that you have to throw your drawers at brothers, just get out of the marriage for crying out loud. Being married before, I would never want to be part of the cause of destroying someone's marriage. What comes around goes around.

Don't get me wrong, aggression has its place, so I am kind of used to it, but still quite shocked when a woman, in my opinion, has it going on comes on to me. I'm usually saying to myself, "Wow, you mean to tell me you're not married or dating?" I'm talking super fine, saved, educated and everything else. This really goes to show me how huge the deficit is among men and women. There are some women that have to help a brother along the way who may not get it because of his own naivety. Believe it or not, in the Bible, it was Ruth that stepped to Boaz. What I'm saying is that there are some women that will never step to a man because she may be old-fashioned or think she is too good to pursue a man.

Marriage is Honorable

When I spoke in Louisville, Kentucky, a few years ago, a young lady approached me after the service. She pulled me to the side and told me that she enjoyed oral sex with her husband, but her pastor said that it was wrong. The next words she said dumbfounded me.

I'm not sure of the motives of this woman but this has to go on the list of the most unusual questions I've been asked. Certain scenarios I never found myself in until I was divorced. I really at times felt like a huge target with a bull's eye on my chest! Was it simply because a wedding ring wasn't on my finger? Who knows.

"So what should I do, preacher?" she said.

I hear so many divorced people in church speak on when they get married again how things will be so much different this time around. Only divorced people will understand this type of talk, but the second time around there are some things you will not tolerate, period. When I counsel couples that have sex problems such as one is not giving it up to the other I am shocked. In a time in day where your spouse would say to you I'm not going to do this or that sexually, things can get confusing. I know some of you may not agree with that but you don't wait until you turn a person out then marry them and say I'm not going to do those things anymore. You should say all that BEFORE you marry them and give them the benefit to say if that's what they want. However, keep in mind that biblically you shouldn't be sexing before marriage anyway.

I respect pastors and the rules established for their congregation. I did not want to negate his instruction, but I didn't want her husband waiting for me in the parking lot either. I'll treat the balance of our conversation as a patient-therapist session and not divulge the details of my advice.

As a member of a church presided by Bishop Buck wild, his teachings on marital sex may be based on the following Scripture:

> *Marriage is honorable in all and the bed undefiled.*
>
> Hebrews 13:4

His philosophy: do what pleases you as long as you both consent to it, whereas, Bishop Boring adheres to missionary-position-only sex. From his perspective, all else is taboo and an abomination to God. It's amazing how I've witnessed married couples give their spiritual leaders the control over their own bedrooms. It's even worse when church women let their pastor tell them what to do sexually with their unsaved husbands. And you wonder why he won't come to church? What man wants to sit down and hear another man preach that's controlling what goes down in his bedroom? I know I don't! Do you satisfy your companion's desires to keep your marriage flourishing or do you let your pastor run your master bedroom? Think about it.

A Human Magnet

When I was married I guess I had blinders on because I didn't really see the advances of women as I do now.

As a traveling minister, I had no idea that speaking to a congregation of believers was an aphrodisiac for some women. I'm still not clear why a man of God bringing forth the Word is sexually arousing – an obvious woman thing – but I've been told that a preacher's tone, moves and sweat stimulate women. They daydream about intimate relations while he's winding up his homiletics. Of course I'm not talking about every woman in the church. There are some sanctified women that can solely hear the word he's preaching, even if he looks like Denzel Washington.

Being divorced made it difficult at times by all the attention I was getting. I got winks, lip-licking and uncrossed legs while I preached the gospel. The behavior became the norm. I received as many offers for sex as I did for a glass of water.

It is common for women to follow the car of the preacher after church to find out the hotel in which he's staying. Crazy, but true. I've checked into many hotels using an alias to maintain privacy.

Thank God for my father's leadership and a consistent prayer life. I needed both to dodge the advances. The attraction had nothing to do with my physical attributes or evangelistic savvy, but rather the enemy's attempts to thwart my purpose and make a mockery of God.

Some men use their influence to pick up women. I am by no means a goody-two-shoes – some days are better than others – but manipulation has never been my proclivity. Thank the Lord!

It is not the absence of a wedding ring, but the anointing that creates the magnetism. What some women don't know is that most preachers have PMS – prophetic mood swings. We can drive a sister nuts. Ask any first lady.

Masturbation

This thought may seem quite out of place for many readers but I'll show you how relevant it is. If you are divorced and are trying to live holy that means you are not having sex. You still with me? There are many that may not be having sex but yet they are getting off nightly! If you were a person that masturbated heavy as a youth and especially before getting in church that's a serious habit that can come back after divorce.

While no specific Scripture exists on self-gratification, doctrines regarding masturbation vary. On countless occasions, I've been asked if it is acceptable to masturbate to avoid fornication. One school of thought teaches that as long as you do not involve another person, you are free to pleasure your flesh. But what about sinning against your body?

> *For ye are bought with a price: therefore glorify God in your body, and in your spirit, which are God's.*
>
> I Corinthians 6:20

If you fantasize about a partner while you masturbate, haven't you sinned?

> *But I say unto you, that whosoever looketh on a woman to lust after her hath committed adultery with her already in his heart.*
>
> Matthew 5:28

In one of the seminars I conduct around the country, I was stumped when asked the question concerning masturbation in a way I never heard it. "What if your spouse travels and in a moment of loneliness during the night you began thinking about them and proceed to masturbate? Have you then sinned? Hmmmm…I'll save that one for my Bishop.

When it's been so long since you've had a release, sometimes it feels like your body has a mind of its own. Going home at night by yourself, you decide to turn on the television to wind down and relax and you find out that was the biggest set up. The hard way I found out that HBO is really Hells Best Option, Cinemax can cause you to Sin to the Max, and ShowTime can leave God with no time.

With sex in your heart and fantasies bombarding your thoughts, the continual longing intensifies. Like Pandora's Box – once opened it is difficult to shut – masturbation often leads to sex with a partner. It's impossible to pleasure yourself constantly and never desire a person there with you. The highest fulfillment of sex is not just pleasing yourself but your mate. Masturbation should not be an option because it will make you worse in the end. Masturbation is a mousetrap with a good piece of cheese on it. It opens you up to watching pornographic movies, the lust on the Internet, sex-crazed chat lines, and eventually someone in your bed. Trust me some doors are better shut than open. What takes a minute to open will take a few years to close.

CHAPTER 9

. . . .

Should I Look For Another or Stay By Myself?

I have asked myself and have been asked this same question by others on a constant basis. The answer changes depending on what's going on in my life and in the lives of others around me. In a time when people are connecting for all the wrong reasons: loneliness, desperation, parenting assistance and finances, I recognized that loneliness for a season is far better than misery for a lifetime.

I have witnessed humdrum relationships that led to affairs, pornography addictions or two people coexisting under one roof. At the sports bar, he's watching the game, while she's chatting on her cell phone. In the mall, he's heading to Radio Shack, while she's rushing to Macy's. They coordinate a meeting time and place as if they were on a field trip. They might as well be alone by the way they disregard each other's presence as their relationship has become predictable and monotonous.

The challenge is to have patience to deal with the season of loneliness whether six months or six years. Dating can be interesting and fascinating: meeting people from different backgrounds, going to new places and dining at exquisite restaurants. Those things can keep you dating for years, only if it went like that. No one talks about the idiosyncrasies hidden in the middle. You don't know that he rented the BMW or that she's still dating a felon who has been following you and her all night. Or what about the 40-year-old brother who took the pictures off the wall before you came over so you wouldn't know that he lives with his mother?

If you don't have discernment, you can burn out quickly. My father used to ask me, "Why continue to date someone with whom you know you have no future?" Being honest with myself I have to admit some things were lost in the fire and I greatly struggle with trust issues. I constantly ask the good Lord to give me the strength to trust again.

People will date you, spend your money and run you across town on errands, all the while knowing you are a temporary stand-in until the real mate comes along. One of the most sincere things an individual can do is set the boundaries at the beginning of the relationship. Be honest about your intentions whether you're looking for occasional companionship or a lifelong commitment.

Let me caution you. Although you state and reiterate your plan, after a few dates, it is not uncommon for feelings to supersede logic. That's when problems arise. As a mature adult, you may have to put your feelings in check and say, "I need to abort this relationship because I'm getting in over my head."

Don't look for the other person to control the relationship. If your feelings have unleashed and you don't harness the reigns, you will get hurt. An immature individual will accuse the other person of "playing with my emotions" and place the blame on the wrong party. One psychologist said, "When a person tells you how they feel, believe them." I agree.

I experienced the excruciating pain of rejection when my ex-wife first asked for a divorce. I thought we could work through our differences. I got on my knees and begged her to stay. Her refusal was one of the most hurtful blows to my ego. Even as I wrote this chapter – years after the divorce – I cringe at the memory. A spirit of rejection came upon me causing me to terminate many blossoming relationships. I'm sure my abrupt actions left some wondering, "What in the world did I do wrong?"

They That Wait Upon the Lord

I learned to wait. Time allowed me to endure special days, holidays and celebrations alone. I used the time to develop, grow and understand me.

Recently I went to lunch with the most beautiful woman ever. She was saved, good morals, good credit, smart, savvy, a leader, submissive, and gave you a piece of her mind at the right time. I would marry her tomorrow...if she wasn't my momma (LOL)! I don't care what nobody says my lady will have to possess some of the characteristics of my mom.

My mother taught me how to cook, bake and fry chicken, macaroni and cheese, pecan cornbread and more. I enjoyed the delight in my sons' eyes when they came home from school and inhaled the aroma of homemade dinner. Pride engulfed me when they requested specific meals I had prepared, especially fried fish. I designated Wednesday nights as Mexican Night with fajitas, tacos and picante sauce.

I have always taken my mother out to lunch; however, following the divorce, our excursions were like counseling sessions. If you want to know about women, talk to a woman and likewise for men. My mother imparted fresh wisdom. She told me that a man should not be totally dependent on a woman for anything but reproduction. Know how to wash your clothes, clean your home, iron and plant flowers in a garden if that's your thing. I believe she could have been a psychiatrist or hosted a talk show.

As the light that once shined brightly, again peeked from my soul, I asked the question: why take the actions of one woman out on all women? I have a better understanding about women. For example, it's natural for a woman to want – and expect – security from a man, a sense of belonging.

For years, I pondered whether I was willing to risk rejection again. The potential for a relationship to end on bad terms is ever prevalent. Fear of failure stands side-by-side with rejection. This spirit must be conquered by the Word of God and prayer. Rejection is not a bad thing if your desires are not the desires God has for you. I'm learning that man's rejection is God's protection. Our finite minds cannot conceptualize that his omniscience means that he's looking out for our best interest even though we can't see the future.

I know church girls who are attracted to thugs. Only after they acted upon the attraction and attached to the hoodlums did they realize the mistake. God caused that thug to reject you because his next woman received a three-year prison sentence for carrying drugs in her car. It could have been you. I have friends who have been rejected by women – whom they loved and cherished – for someone who made more money. Once they got over the humiliation and hurt, they realized that God did them a favor. Who wants a gold digger as a companion?

It took me three years to thank my ex-wife for divorcing me. Her actions made me the man I am today, better and 10 times stronger. Stop crying and stressing about who rejected you, it was part of God's plan to make you better, not bitter.

Life After a Painful Divorce

Your heart may be broken in a hundred pieces because of the person who left you for someone else, but I dare you to keep living. You will see that it was a backdoor blessing. Take that pain and make it work for you. Draw something positive from the relationship: a better understanding of your expectations, a different way to communicate, and a third-eye vision for spotting future counterfeits. Since it didn't destroy you, it served to make you stronger.

Do me a favor: put down this book and write a note to someone who rejected you. In a sweet spirit – no sarcasm – thank that person for the times you had. Indicate something positive that you learned during the relationship. Express how you are excited about the next chapter in your life. Purge yourself of the baggage of unfinished business. You can forward the note to them or discard it. It's the act of releasing the pain and taking back your peace of mind that's essential to this favor. I promise the lightened burden will feel like you dropped a backpack of bricks after a three-mile hike…up hill. Keep in mind that if you feel the urge to cuss them out or belittle their character, you are not ready to do me this favor. Take more time to heal and regroup.

Getting Back Into the Dating Game

Some people say that opposites attract, but they can also attack. When individuals try to get to know one another, it is an exchange of information. You are finding out new and different things about that person. Sometimes their lifestyle is in total contrast to yours, interesting at first but can later become a source of contention if you are not open for change. It is unfair to put enormous expectations on a person to change to accommodate your preferences. Change occurs from the inside out and only if desired by the changer.

I'm learning that many people live within parenthesis. They seldom leave their side of town, go to the same grocery store, shop at the same malls, etc. Creatures of habit confined within a self-imposed box. I know people who take the same route to and from work, never venturing a different way for a change of scenery.

If you connect with someone you like but don't like their ways, problems will arise. Anyone can act like they enjoy your lifestyle when what they enjoy is you. The two likes are not the same. For example, he is into horror and action movies, when you enjoy romance and comedies. Your initial fondness for him will have you seated in the theatre shielding your eyes and screaming when the slow-running woman falls for the fifth time and the ax-wielding psychopath slices her like a tomato. But after a few decapitations and dismemberments, you encourage him to see that with his friends. Many men – me included – do not like to go shopping with women – mother, sister or girlfriend. Deception will have me at the mall with her, full smile, carrying bags, as if I'm enjoying our fellowship. Eight months later, when I have been in every store at least 10 times, I express my true feelings. From her perspective, I have changed, when in fact, I'm reverting to my true self. If you don't care for certain things, let it be known up front.

Flaws and All

Some differences are manageable while others are unacceptable to you. Should you accept flaws and all? A classy woman would not tolerate an unmannered man. His lack of etiquette would cause her too much embarrassment. A financially astute man will not struggle in a relationship with a woman who spends her mortgage money on stilettos and weekly hair appointments.

I have a friend who had taken his girl-friend and her son to the movies. In route to the theatre, her son kicked the back of the driver's seat in rhythm with the music. He waited to see if his date would correct her child, but she said nothing. Fifteen minutes into the kangarooing, he turned down the music and asked her to have her son stop. She copped an attitude, took on the sister-girl posture and said, "He's only a child, so stop tripping." My friend was driving a $60,000 S-Class Mercedes with six motors in the seat. But even if he had a Chevy Chevette, the fact that his woman-friend did not require her son to respect his property remained. This incident led to their breakup.

A major flaw many daters overlook, because they are so caught up in each other, is the flaw of children. Before you turn me off, let me clarify. Studies have been proven that children can be the main reason for the demise of a relationship. Discipline, differing expectations, child support and dealing with the drama of the other parent can run off the weak at heart. If these components are not addressed, the relationship is doomed.

Allergic to Kids

If you have children and the person you are dating acts allergic to them, that's a serious problem. How do you overcome that hurdle? The opposing sides should be a deal breaker, but some people are so preoccupied with companionship that they allow their children to be mistreated. I know a guy whose new wife told him that his 12-year-old daughter could visit for a few hours but never spend the night. He agreed, despite the fact that they have two spare bedrooms and a huge backyard. A parent who allows this type of treatment is not worthy of a child.

Dating a person who also has kids can be a plus as they are more apt to understand the dynamics of effective parenting. Plans change in a matter of minutes because a child has a stomachache or the babysitter forgot you needed her services. If you have well-mannered children and your love interest doesn't care for children, like a doctor in the delivery room holding a newborn, cut the cord.

How Bad Do You Want It?

"How bad do you want it?" is a viable question that must be asked in your quest for companionship. Will you accept a studio apartment, tolerate a 20-year-old hoopty or endure cheap polyester clothes off the clearance rack? Or do you draw the line at a three-bedroom house, a BMW and custom-tailored clothes? Most never ask that question because they think that love is sufficient.

Some people are content living at the bottom of the barrel, while others never settle for second best. Is this conundrum love or war? Your aspirations, goals and ambitions need to be comparable for the relationship to flourish. You need to consider where that person is today, where they desire to be in the future and how they fit into your plans. What's wrong with wanting to live in a $400,000 house if you're willing to work for it? Is it wrong to want three automobiles or vacation four weeks a year? Don't connect with someone who's content living with a basement mentality, when God has ordained you to possess the penthouse.

Cleanliness is Next to Godliness

Psychologists say that if you want to know whether or not you can get along with a person, live with them. You would never know that the man who picks you up in a clean car with polished shoes, a fresh haircut and minty-fresh breath, keeps his house in such disarray that it needs to be condemned. French-tip nails, red lipstick and green eye shadow can mask her unkempt house that wreaks of two-week-old dishes, piles of dirty clothes and used kitty litter.

Cleanliness is next to Godliness. It's not a Scripture but it's true nonetheless. You can have enough love in your relationship to fill every cabin on the Love Boat, but if your love interest has bad living habits, you're in for a rumble in the jungle.

I had a friend who didn't like going home because his house was filthy. He refused to make love to his wife until she cleaned the house. That's crazy.

Know what you're working with. Stop by unannounced to see how they keep their house, well maybe not, it depends on the flow of your relationship. Anyone can clean up when they know you're visiting, but what about when they aren't expecting you? Can you live with a man who leaves his underwear on the living room floor, lets the trash can flow over like Niagara Falls and only flushes when he defecates? I know it's a little disgusting, but I know a guy with the toilet mentality: If it's yellow, let it mellow. If it's brown, flush it down. Yuck!

Once, I used the bathroom in the home of a female friend and her sink had so much hair in it that it looked like a chia pet got a haircut!

On the other end of the spectrum, we have the super clean freaks: obsessed with cleaning to the point that it becomes unbearable. Vacuuming the same room four times a day to remove footprints or emptying the trash when a paper towel is dropped in it can be a bit much. Look for balance in someone with habits similar to yours. The commonality does not mean that things will flow smoothly, but at least you have minimized a potential source of disruption.

Committing Again

Committing when so many options are presented is difficult. Think of it as being confined in a town jail when cowboys, saloons and gunfights were prevalent. The sheriff's feet are propped on the desk. His head bobs as he nods off to sleep. You see your chance for freedom on the wall where the cell keys hang on a hook just beyond your reach. Who wants to be chained to the wrong person when the possibility of mutual fulfillment is inches away? I realize that I may never get everything I want from one woman, however some things are non-negotiable. (See the chapter "Are you ready to love again).

At times, my desire is to remain single. The freedom to come and go at my discretion is attractive. Bringing a wife into the picture can lead to disagreements about time, interests and money. I am comfortable watching every televised sporting event on my big screen television with the volume on blast, eating dinner without vegetables and sleeping across the width of my bed.

The singleness decision can put a man on the top of every woman's list. Women can be quite aggressive and that posturing feeds the flames of an already hot situation. To the single and ready-to-mingle crew, be true, honest and forthright with whom you are dating. If you play games be prepared for the penalty: sugar in the gas tank, key scratched car, a brick through the window, harassing phone calls and more. If you don't see the relationship going any further than an occasional casual dinner, make that known in the beginning.

Some daters are too impatient to take the time to get to know you and let you know them. A third-date female said to me, "You need to tell me now; where is this relationship going?"

I was quite shocked and disturbed with her comment so I honestly responded and said, "To a movie and then getting some chicken wings." No fourth date with her. When a person is moving that fast, it causes caution and concern. I have been taught that time will expose a person what 20 detectives could never find out.

From my experience, some women read more into a friendship than men. He invites her to a family function to hang out and she perceives it as acceptance into the family. He asks her to join him for dinner (he has to eat so why not have some company?), she considers it a date.

I recommend an outing to the movies or a not-so-quaint restaurant in the platonic, friendly, get-to-know-this-person phase of the relationship to keep things impersonal.

To avoid the deadly descent into the abyss of craziness, even when a man is bored and she wants to connect daily, don't walk toward the light. Once you set a precedence of routine time together – in person, by telephone or text – be mindful that your "friend" may equate time spent as a call for commitment. Let your words and actions complement each other and convey your intentions on a regular basis. Otherwise, he or she may accuse you of leading them on. This technique may not work for everyone, which is why you have the option of filing a restraining order. Now that's funny.

CHAPTER 10

· · · · · · · · · · · · · · · · ·

We Can Make It Work

Can I Divorce-Proof My Marriage?

Ultimately, only God knows if a marriage is divorce proof as only He can look into the heart. For whatever reason, many people – especially Christians – believe that marriage generates an automatic divorce-proof mechanism. Whether faith or ignorance, they do not expect their marriage to fail and so they do not put adequate effort into making it succeed. The end result, as stated earlier, is an abnormally high incidence of divorce in Christian marriages. Like a scout trekking the marshes as front man for his platoon, they were ambushed by enemies camouflaged and laying in wait.

> *But he that is married careth for the things that are of the world, how he may please his wife.*
>
> I Corinthians 7:33

As quiet as it's kept, marriage is not all about you. Rather it is about how much you can care for and love your spouse. If all married persons were giving and unselfish with respect to their mates, the divorce rate would plummet.

I meet single people who have developed a list of stipulations for their pending prisoner – I mean, partner. With preconceived notions and limitations on the depth of their love, they have plagued the relationship before it begins.

A successful marriage is without barriers. How can two become one with mountains of differences distancing them?

Like Christ loves us without limits, so should you love your mate. Be willing to do whatever it takes to support, love and satisfy your mate or do not get married. You are not ready if your needs supersede those of your partner.

Expert marriage counselors give two main reasons for the infidelity of men: they are not stimulated in the bedroom or the boardroom.

The bedroom is self-explanatory: we want what we want, when we want it. Some women tend to give what they want, when they want and how they want to give it. If a man asks for a glass of orange juice and you give him a glass of milk, have you met his need? Sure, he may no longer be thirsty, but the desire has not been quenched.

Sex should never be held from either person. I know women would say a man shouldn't withhold emotional affection and they are right. I can only speak from a man's perspective because I am one. Some wives will withhold sex because the hubby is not doing his part: paying the bills, being faithful, showing affection etc. Of course and unfortunately you have some wives that still withhold sex as a weapon to get what she wants. This is a major no-no! I'm talking in this context to the husband that is doing his part. I heard one older woman say "if you feed the dog at home he rarely roams!"

The boardroom equates to the emotional needs of a man – that's right, men have feelings too. A man wants to feel like the king of the jungle, the leader of the pack, the head of his home. He wants his wife to admire him, adore him and stroke his ego on occasion. God wired us this way. That's why He commanded women to reverence their husbands in Ephesians 5. A man's need to be revered or respected is like a woman's need to be loved. Without it, we are empty.

As creatures of habit, it is difficult to modify behavior once it has been reinforced by repetition. However, marriage is about flexibility. Forget the cliché: it's a give and take. Give without concern for the return and watch what happens.

So can you divorce-proof your marriage? Open communication, quality time and selflessness are great tools to safeguard your marriage, but only God knows the intent of the heart. Seek Him diligently. Ask Him to show you the heart of your beloved and once He exposes the truth, believe it.

CHAPTER 11

Are You Ready to Love Again?

On the 13th anniversary of my wedding, July 25, my divorce was final. The day it began was the same day it ended. Interesting, huh? My lifelong commitment to love, honor and respect, began and ended on the same day.

Someone asked, "If you had to do it all over again, would you?"

Without hesitation, I said, "Yes." Despite the heartache, the marriage had high points: two wonderful sons, a deeper knowledge of self, good people on her side of the family, and more. No matter how bad your divorce may have been, it's certainly not enough to make you give up on true love.

Forgiveness

I do not harbor any ill feelings. My ex-wife and I have our moments, but overall it's good. We chose to maintain a mature relationship for our children. We collectively decided that our sons deserved two civil parents who could be in the same room without arguing or "showing out" all while expressing unconditional love for them. We made sure that the boys understood the divorce was not their fault. It took some time, but the sadness I once saw in my sons' eyes is gone. I like that. No, I love that.

There may be a few people that when you were going through your transition they may have said some things that they shouldn't have said. You never know what people heard concerning your situation and sad to say it's easier to believe a lie than the truth! But remember this: Be careful what you say about your enemies. You never know, you just might become their friend again. Forgiveness is one of the most powerful tools you need to bounce back.

The Transition

My ex-wife has since left Christianity. She studies Islam and is now Muslim. I wondered if she ever believed like I did – given the bipolarization between doctrines – but left that judgment for the Lord. The boys complain because they are not allowed to order pepperoni or sausage on pizza when they are with her, but they make up for it when they get with me. I have no problem with pork on my fork (lol). The pork matter sounds trivial, but it's the subtle and often overlooked differences that can hinder the transition even between amicable parents.

The mind is an amazing organ. It adapts to overwhelming situations, and by the grace of God, makes you do the seemingly impossible. Many people told me that they could not have endured a divorce without unleashing rage or numbing the pain with alcohol and drugs. The best lesson I learned about love and women is that you never know what you can endure until you have to endure it. And because I'm a fast learner, the mistakes that I made out of ignorance and immaturity will not be repeated.

Looking For Love

Should the Lord opt for me to marry again, I will not jump into it in the hopes that she has the potential to meet my needs and will change in the areas that lack. I have assessed some characteristics – must haves and preferences.

— A communicator. My lady friend has to be open to interactive dialogue. Not one who shuts down and locks me out when shes upset. Communication means to reach a common ground or level of understanding. That cannot happen if one of the two involved is not engaged in the discussion.

— Submissive. The 10-letter profane word that women dread and some men abuse. Submission is biblical and reciprocal: Submit yourselves one to another, so why shy away from it? Im not looking to launch an argument over every decision. Loud, overbearing, bossy is not a fit for me. Can she be assertive? Yes. Overly aggressive? Not in the least. A refined, witty woman who can get what she wants without putting her hands on her hips and her finger in my face. Remember how our grandmothers, mothers and aunties used to do it? They're husbands used to walk around the house like the king of the jungle, beating his chest but at the end of the day he always did what she said. That's a smart woman, a real smart woman.

— Feminine. I am a saved man, but a man nonetheless. I want my woman to look like a woman. Her sway, her scent, her hair. W-o-m-a-n. Enough said.

— Giving. My lady has to have a giving spirit that includes understanding and responding to my needs: giving me what I want and not what she wants me to have.

— Secure. My wife needs to know that shes all I want and need. By the time I lavish her with my kindness, affection and whatever else makes her feel loved, she will not have to question her position as my one and only.

— Alive. No, not as in breathing, but living life. As a speaker, I am on the go quite a bit. I need my woman to have a life that fulfills and occupies her. I am not built to have someone follow me around like a parole officer. Of course our life together will be top priority, but I want her to have interests of her own.

— Employment. Lord, please let her have a job and accomplishments beyond a lofty wardrobe. My bachelor friends explained that a woman who has not acquired anything is a shell woman. She is shaped just right, long hair, perfect complexion, sexy smile, yet she has no money, no job, lives with three girlfriends in a two-bedroom apartment and has a funky attitude. Taking on the form of woman-ness, but denying the virtue thereof. This type of woman is dateable when youre bored but shed never get a chance to meet your church family and definitely not your mother. Her value is limited to one room of the house and I do not mean the kitchen.

— Good credit and respectable children— along with appealing physical attributes—round out my wonderful woman.

— God-fearing. My betrothed must have a personal relationship with the Lord that permeates throughout her life. A worshipper at church, home and work. I am in church every Sunday and oftentimes a few days through the week. The relationship won't work if I want to worship and she wants to club it. What would make matters worse would be that she is only in church because of me. I wouldn't want a woman in my life that I would have to beg and nag just to serve God. Without God in her life, any hope of a happy marriage is out of the question.

> *Favor is deceitful and beauty is vain, but a woman that feareth the Lord shall be praised.*
>
> Proverbs 30:31

To some it may be a lot to ask, but since I'm going to wait, I might as well wait for what I want.

Three days after I met one young lady, she said, "I'm so glad I met you. I'm three months behind on my car note."

With my eyebrows raised, I said, "And what does that have to do with me?"

How is it that some women want a commitment but have nothing to commit to? Finding a woman who wants you for you, and not what you have, is harder than finding a pair of Prada's at Kmart.

I understand that most women want security, but when a man sets the table with plates and silverware and she doesn't bring anything for the meal but an appetite, it doesn't make for a good presentation.

Men are even receptive to a progressive woman who has not yet "arrived." Attending college or trade school, repairing her credit or in a first-time homebuyer's program speaks volumes. Working toward improvement is a turn on for me. Simply put, the woman I can't see myself living without is the woman I will marry.

The Bounce-Back Factor

Through hard work and the blessings of God I have rebounded in several aspects. Financially, I make on-time mortgage payments and have three reliable vehicles – all paid in full.

My boys have the same pre-divorce bedrooms with Fathead posters of their favorite athletes plastered on the walls. They still shoot hoops on the basketball court in the yard, and for eight years running, we take an annual summer vacation to Orlando, Florida.

I'm enjoying more personal travel, too. New York, Detroit and Atlanta are my favorite destinations and I recently added a new outlet – scuba diving. Scuba diving in Barbados is one of the most exhilarating things I have ever experienced.

My favorite spot is the backyard gazebo; lying in my lounge chair with the fireplace simmering.

I've learned on this page of my life to protect myself from drama, stress, and straight up foolishness. People can decide to call you, but you ultimately decide to answer. Never lose your power of choice.

But my most prized possession is peace of mind. I have never expected to have true peace given the trauma and drama of the divorce. From the other side of understanding, I encourage you to seek peace above everything else and the rest will follow.

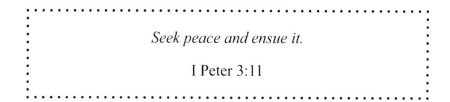

> *Seek peace and ensue it.*
>
> I Peter 3:11

The following three points have put a smile on my face, hope in my heart and reassurance in my spirit:

1. Accept what has happened.
2. Let it go.
3. Believe the best is yet to come.

When you accept the situation, you align yourself with the will of God. While in prayer, God said to me, "I allowed it because I knew you could handle it."

Whether you have been fired, evicted or your children are on assignment from Satan, God knew it before it happened and still allowed it. Destiny does not only work for good things, but the bad also. A drive-by shooting, a home invasion or an18th-month stint in jail is part of your destiny, if God allows it.

I once said, "I wish I had never married."

God asked me, "Do you really believe that?" Of course, He knew the answer. I believe that He wanted me to hear how foolish I sounded.

I picked up my cell phone, looked at my sons on the screensaver and said, "Lord, I hear you." If life experiences form character, then you must ask: was it worth it? Absolutely. What makes me jump out of bed without an alarm clock? The answer is that the knowledge that something better is in my future.

Somewhere someone is moving into their dream home,

opening a business, driving off the lot in a new vehicle or marrying their soul mate. If it's happening to someone, why can't it happen to you? God walked you through it and the best is yet to come. Receive it. You survived a momentous life-changing event. Walk tall, chest out, head high, shoulders squared, because you are a survivor. Live knowing that your happiness is not determined by a ring on your finger or by who has left your life. Your happiness is in knowing that you are here for a reason. Not to just endure pain and suffering, but to have joy and happiness. And after coming through a rough season, you certainly qualify for years of smooth sailing on a boat named Peace. Ride on my friends and know that there is Life After a Painful Divorce.

About Jonathan K. Sanders

One of eight children born to Bishop Fred and Esther Sanders, Jonathan realized there was a call on his life at an early age. Even though the enemy planned to deter the young evangelist from reaching his destiny, God's plan would ultimately prevail.

After years of struggling with drugs, alcohol abuse and crime, the Lord delivered Jonathan through a revival conducted by his father Apostle Fred Sanders, on September 28, 1990, in Detroit, Michigan. J. K. Sanders' unique deliverance ministry has transformed lives and caused souls to be set free. Anointed with the gift of prophecy, he utters the oracles of God with accuracy. His intense delivery of the Gospel will grip your spirit and challenge your intellect with Sermon's such as: I Survived a Bad Experience and How to Act When Under Attack.

A living testimony that the power of God can deliver and transform, he preaches the Gospel with authority, standing boldly on his favorite Scripture: What shall we then say to these things? If God be for us, who can be against us? ~Romans 8:31

For more information about Jonathan K. Sanders visit
JKSandersMinistries.org
FaceBook.com/JonathanKSanders

For speaking engagements or to order additional copies of
Life After a Painful Divorce
Jonathan K Sanders Ministries, LLC
1933 East Dublin Granville Road #237
Columbus, Ohio 43229
614.840.9141
JKSandersMinistries.org
JSanders1718@yahoo.com
* * * * * * * * * * * * * * * * * *
Please mail _____ copies of
Life After a Painful Divorce

_____
Name

_____
Address

_____
City / State / Zip

(_____)_____
Phone

_____
Email

Quantity Price Per Book Total $14.95
Sales Tax (Ohio residents add $1.05 per book)
Shipping ($1.99 first book, $0.99 each additional)

Grand Total* _____

(Payable to: Jonathan K. Sanders)
Certified check and money orders only